RENEWALS 458-4574
DATE DUE

DEC 3 1			
GAYLORD			PRINTED IN U.S.A.

Portraits and Elegies

Gjertrud Schnackenberg

PORTRAITS AND
ELEGIES

DAVID R. GODINE · BOSTON

A Godine Poetry Chapbook
Fourth Series

First published in 1982 by
DAVID R. GODINE, PUBLISHER, INC.
306 Dartmouth Street
Boston, Massachusetts 02116

Library of Congress Cataloging in Publication Data

Schnackenberg, Gjertrud.
 Portraits and elegies.

 (A Godine poetry chapbook; 4th ser.)
 I. Title.
PS3569.C5178P6   811'.54   80-39824
ISBN 0-87923-368-0

Some of the poems in this book first appeared in the follow-
ing publications: *The Carolina Quarterly, The Kenyon Review,
The Mississippi Review, Ploughshares, The Pushcart Prize, IV.*

"Nightfishing," "Intermezzo," "Walking Home," and
"There are no dead" first appeared in *Poetry.*

Printed in the United States of America

*For my mother
and in memory of my father*

Contents

LAUGHING WITH ONE EYE

Walter Charles Schnackenberg
Professor of History
(1917-1973)

> *And call those works extravagance of breath*
> *That are not suited for such men as come*
> *Proud, open-eyed and laughing to the tomb.*
> W. B. Yeats, "Vacillation"

1. Nightfishing

The kitchen's old-fashioned planter's clock portrays
A smiling moon as it dips down below
Two hemispheres, stars numberless as days,
And peas, tomatoes, onions, as they grow
Under that happy sky; but, though the sands
Of time put on this vegetable disguise,
The clock covers its face with long, thin hands.
Another smiling moon begins to rise.

We drift in the small rowboat an hour before
Morning begins, the lake weeds grown so long
They touch the surface, tangling in an oar.
You've brought coffee, cigars, and me along.
You sit still as a monument in a hall,
Watching for trout. A bat slices the air
Near us, I shriek, you look at me, that's all,
One long sobering look, a smile everywhere
But on your mouth. The mighty hills shriek back.
You turn back to the lake, chuckle, and clamp
Your teeth on your cigar. We watch the black
Water together. Our tennis shoes are damp.
Something moves on your thoughtful face, recedes.

1

Here, for the first time ever, I see how,
Just as a fish lurks deep in water weeds,
A thought of death will lurk deep down, will show
One eye, then quietly disappear in you.
It's time to go. Above the hills I see
The faint moon slowly dipping out of view,
Sea of Tranquility, Sea of Serenity,
Ocean of Storms . . . You start to row, the boat
Skimming the lake where light begins to spread.
You stop the oars, mid-air. We twirl and float.

I'm in the kitchen. You are three days dead.
A smiling moon rises on fertile ground,
White stars and vegetables. The sky is blue.
Clock hands sweep by it all, they twirl around,
Pushing me, oarless, from the shore of you.

2. *Intermezzo*

Steinway in German script above the keys,
Letters like dragons curling stiff gold tails,
Gold letters, ivory keys, the black wood cracked
By years of sunlight, into dragon scales.
Your music breathed its fire into the room.
We'd hear jazz sprouting thistles of desire,
Or jazz like the cat's cry from beneath
The passing tire, when you played the piano
Afternoons; or 'Au Clair de la Lune.'
Scarlatti's passages fluttered like pages.
Sometimes you turned to Brahms, a depth, more true,
You studied him to find out how he turned
Your life into a memory for you.

In Number 6 of Opus 118,
Such brief directions, Andante, sotto voce:
The opening notes like single water drops
Each with an oceanic undertow
That pulled you deeper even as you surfaced
Hundreds of miles from where the first note drew
You in, and made your life a memory,
Something that happened long ago to you.

And through that Intermezzo you could see
As through a two-way mirror until it seemed
You looked back at your life as at a room,
And saw those images that would compose
Your fraction of eternity, the hallway
In its absolute repose, the half-lit room,
The drapes at evening holding the scent of heat,
The marble long-lost under the piano,
A planet secretive, cloud-wrapped and blue,
Silent and gorgeous by your foot, making
A god lost in reflection, a god of you.

3. *Walking Home*

Walking home from school one afternoon,
Slightly abstracted, what were you thinking of?
Turks in Vienna? Luther on Christian love?
Or were you with Van Gogh beneath the moon
With candles in his hatband, painting stars
Like singed hairs spinning in a candle flame?
Or giant maps where men take, lose, reclaim
Whole continents with pins? Or burning cars
And watchtowers and army-censored news
In Chile, in the Philippines, in Greece,
Colonels running the universities,
Assassinations, executions, coups—

You walked, and overhead some pipsqueak bird
Flew by and dropped a lot of something that
Splattered, right on the good professor, splat.
Now, on the ancient Rhine, so Herod heard,
The old Germanic chieftains always read
Such droppings as good luck: opening the door,
You bowed to improve my view of what you wore,
So luckily, there on the center of your head.

Man is not a god, that's what you said
After your heart gave out, to comfort me
Who came to comfort you but sobbed to see
Your heartbeat blipping on a TV overhead.
You knew the world was in a mess, and so,
By God, were you; and yet I never knew
A man who loved the world as much as you,
And that love was the last thing to let go.

4. A Dream

Death makes of your abandoned face
A secret house an empty place
And I come back wanting that much
To ask you to come back I touch

The door where are you it's so black
The taste of smoke is smoke I back
Away when creeping lines of fire
Appear and travel faster higher

Where are you and beneath the floors
God turns the gas jets up and roars
The way flames roar and I should run
And blackness burning like the sun

All empty underneath my hair
I start to chuckle where oh where
My brimming eyes stupid and bland
My grin extending past my hand

5. *Bavaria*

That day in Germany comes back, the deep
Enchanted woods and Castle Neuschwanstein,
A clouded mind's fantastical decline
To fairytale dream halls. The barren steep
Mountain of rock behind the torrent as it drops
To silver thunder, the path of our approach
Built for his French rococo lit-up coach,
Clouds, alps, towers, stack like theater props
Around the locked gates where his guards defied
Psychiatrists from Munich. And as we look
Into a courtyard from a storybook,
You describe what we would find inside:

Romanticism's last hysteria
Of Niebelungen murals golden-iced
Along the Hall of Song, the King with Christ
Floating in gold above Bavaria,
Chambers where every fantasy is wooed,
A cave of artificial stalactites
And waterfalls lit by electric lights,
The Throne Room where, in mountain solitude,

Ludwig the Second works a ouija-board.
His tongue searches a cavity, he relishes
The nerve and pain, das Reich as far off as
The twangling of a cloudscaped harpsichord.
The heroes of the ancient race festoon
This dream theater, this lunatic's refuge
And lovers' hideaway, this whole weird huge
Orbit of Wagner's artificial moon . . .
Cosima sniffs a 'new brutality

In men,' now that Wagner is dead, his music's
Tree of lightning bears a politics
Of acid fruit; and blanket-wrapped Nietzsche
Sees armies marching out of village clocks
From where he sits in Zürich's health resort,
His nightmare coming true, the fresh report
Of shrill fringes expounding paradox
In Viennese cafes, where young men slake
Their power-thirst with 'primacy of will,'
Like heroes, in a castle, on a hill . . .
The Dream King floating face down on the lake.

You say time will be fair, but I see how
The West gathers, how all the diseased West
Could crush you, like a pressure in the chest
Building, decade by decade, toward Dachau,
Toward hiding places flushed by midnight knocks:
A woman bends in futile reflex to
Conceal her wedding diamonds in her shoe,
They hurt her foot, her panicked hand unlocks
The door, she finds, not the police, but her
Sister-in-law, looking left and right,
The coarse face underlined by a soft white
Collar of newly confiscated fur,
The paws intact, 'Still, I've a heart, yes,
That I have,' furtive on the landing.
Now, somewhere the Hangman of Stutthof is handing
A Todeskandidat a paper dress;
As camp by camp the lawless ego maps
The growing territory it proclaims,
A small eraser rubs a list of names
To rubber bits; now, as the Führer naps,
Dreaming of Wild Westerns in his chair

Till early morning, now, in North Berlin,
An apartment building shatters from within,
And, like a tooth, a bathtub dangles there.

We linger, for a moment, at the gates:
Here Ludwig, in his grisly innocence,
Plucked waterlilies planted an hour since
By silent gardeners, hurled his dinner plates
At statue-niches peopled with assassins,
And wept that Nietzsche called his love a Jew.
It is November, 1962,
A siren from the village rises, spins
Itself into a planet of alarm
That hangs a moment in the wilderness,
And dusk comes through the forest with Venus,
Star of emergency, upon its arm.

6. *The Bicyclist*

Crossing a bridge in our VW bus
In Stratford-on-Avon, you swerved but grazed
A skinny man riding a bicycle.
God! Was he mad! You pulled off to the side
Beyond the bridge, and he came after us
Shouting Police! and peddling furiously
In his black suit. You stood by the bus
As he pulled up and flailed at his kickstand
And rained vituperation on your head.
You quietly cut through his narrative,
'Are you all right?' your face kindly and wry.

Through the bus window I saw the moment when
He first saw you, first looked you in the eye.
He straightened up. His hands moved fast
To straighten his bowtie. Well, yes, he supposed
That he was fine. You asked more questions, asked
So quietly I couldn't hear, but I could see
His more emphatically respectful answers
As he began to nod in affirmation
Of all you said. Then he smiled, sort of,
Offering his hand, and when he peddled off
He waved and shouted, Thank you very much!

That's what you were like—you could sideswipe
A bowtied Englishman wobbling across
A narrow bridge on his collapsible bike,
And inspire him, somehow, to thank you for it.

7. *A Dream*

In dreams silent secret and unafraid
I steal away to find you I've divined
Your wish to see me I steal away to find
You in a forest digging with a spade
I touch your shoulder feeling my heart race
To think how glad you'll be but slowly quite
Slowly you turn blindly to me the white
Featureless deep lily of your face

8. *Returning North*

The car lurches on goatpaths,
North and north,
You ask shepherds directions as you drive.
Above the Arctic Circle
Norway's sun rises all night
On you bringing your family on your search
To meet your background face to face.
Your mother left in 1895,
A four-year-old Norwegian, steerage class,
Clutching a copper teapot in the hold,
Her one possession.
At forty-six
You come as a dead sister's only son.

Your aunt waits at a pasture gate,
Holding your letter, looking anxious, small,
Shy as the summer snow
In patches at her feet.
You see your dead mother,
Her hands, her face, her raven hair, her eyes,
You see her hesitate.
She backs away, half-frightened of our car,
And beckons us to follow her
Through cold summer meadows to a barn.
One by one we scale
A ladder and pull ourselves
Up through a hole in the ceiling
Above the pigs and geese,
We have arrived,

And there, lying upon a bed of straw,
A man stares, fever-eyed, then turns away.
Out of respect
The scared, exhilarated family
Hides whispering behind the kitchen door,
Peeking in turns to see
These rich Americans. Two children
Push each other into the room,
Their dialect is difficult for you,
A plate of fish, a plate of goat cheese, bread
Which we are meant to eat in front of them,
Among the coughing and the shining eyes.
This would have been your mother's home.
And we begin to eat
Moments before you realize
The little household is tubercular.

Almost at once, you say that we must go,
There in the mountains
Days and days away,
You say our family is expected
Somewhere else, somewhere immediately,
You ask them to believe
Our visit has been good,
We must go south. They do not understand.
They pull at us, they watch us drive away,
Slowly, painfully south, finding
The way as tears will find their way
Into a mouth, hundreds of miles
To Oslo, the city of clean air
And Lutheran chapels stark, narrow, and pure,

And small, and white,
So like your mother's face.

You said lightly, Forget this incident.
But, father, here, tonight,
It comes to mind
Or my mind comes to it as one winding
Through passageways cut through
Snow-covered sculptured hedges
Comes upon
A waterfall suspended in white frost
And stands amazed and lost, so am I
Lost remembering
The fear crossing your face.

9. *Rome*

You held open the thousand-year-old door
That I might enter in the cold, hushed, dark
Cathedral's cave, that keeps the Bones and Ark,
And, when the eyes adjust, Demon and Whore
Rise on one wall, roaring for Beelzebub
And drag their fingernails through obscene crowds.
But rings of saints chanting in frescoed clouds
Gaze upward from the other wall, they rub
Their fingertips on Mary's hem. You stood
Alone a moment, your figure partly hid
Among those figures; and seeing you amid
That opulence of death, I understood
The wooden crucifix with Christ portrayed
Sagging in fear and in his downcast eyes
His sudden knowledge that to recognize
One's father, father, is to be afraid.

10. *Winter Apples*

I open the kitchen window like an eye:
Our hearts hang in the naked apple boughs
All tumbledown with worms that grind and cry,
Sisters, it's time that one of you takes down

The dead man's clothes blown stiff upon the line.
He isn't here. And now his laughter stops
Rattling the teacups, now his tears, not mine,
Drip from my chin onto the countertop,

Little mirrors of that summertime we saw
An August evening's metamorphosis:
On our hot porch, a snake unhinged his jaw,
A toad half-swallowed in his fatal kiss,

Twin heads and double tongue that cursed our door.
Now apples black with frost cling to the bough,
And all around this house the cold grass stirs
And breathes that frog's blue sob, Oh take me now.

11. A Dream

With shadow ink, on paper that I know
Is shadow, I now make
An Arctic shadow world and ship to take
A last passage. The snow
Breaks up as though the shadow ship were there.
A man leaning against the rail

Watches the twilight North, a wail
Rises around me everywhere,
I realize
What I fear most is true,
That this is you.
And now I want to know, and my voice cries
Crying your name,

You turn to me, and by your look I find
To be alive is to be left behind.
And to be dead, it is the same.
Your pathway closes in the water

Among drifting ice continents.
I want to say you're not alone,
That I am here, to say I am your daughter,
But, instead, I stare the way you stare,

And marveling I watch the face you wear,
Hardened into remote indifference,
Become my own.

12. *"There are no dead"*

Outside a phoebe whistles for its mate,
The rhododendron rubs its leaves against
Your office window: so the Spring we sensed
You wouldn't live to see comes somewhat late.
Here, lying on the desk, your reading glasses,
And random bits of crimped tobacco leaves,
Your jacket dangling its empty sleeves—
These look as if you've just left for your classes.
The chess game is suspended on its board
In your mind's pattern, your wastebasket
Contains some crumpled papers, your filing cabinet
Heavy with years of writing working toward
A metaphysics of impersonal praise.
Here students came and went, here years would draw
Intensities of lines until we saw
Your face beneath an etching of your face.
How many students really cared to solve
History's riddles?—in hundreds on the shelves,
Where men trying to think about themselves
Must come to grips with grief that won't resolve,
Blackness of headlines in the daily news,
And buildings blown away from flights of stairs
All over Europe, tanks in empty squares,
The flaming baby-carriages of Jews.

Behind its glass, a print hangs on the wall,
A detail from the Bayeux Tapestry.
As ignorant women gabbed incessantly,
Their red, sore hands stitched crudely to recall
Forests of ships, the star with streaming hair,
God at Westminster blessing the devout,

They jabbed their thousand needles in and out,
Sometimes too busy talking to repair
The small mistakes; now the centuries of grease
And smoke that stained it, and the blind white moth
And grinning worm that spiraled through the cloth,
Say death alone makes life a masterpiece.

There William of Normandy remounts his horse
A fourth time, four times desperate to drive
Off rumors of his death. His sword is drawn,
He swivels and lifts his visor up and roars,
Look at me well! For I am still alive!
Your glasses, lying on the desk, look on.

DARWIN IN 1881

Sleepless as Prospero back in his bedroom
In Milan, with all his miracles
Reduced to sailors' tales,
He sits up in the dark. The islands loom.
His seasickness upwells,
Silence creeps by in memory as it crept
By him on water, while the sailors slept,
From broken eggs and vacant tortoiseshells.
His voyage around the cape of middle age
Comes, with a feat of insight, to a close,
The same way Prospero's
Ended before he left the stage
To be led home across the blue-white sea,
When he had spoken of the clouds and globe,
Breaking his wand, and taking off his robe:
Knowledge increases unreality.

He quickly dresses.
Form wavers like his shadow on the stair
As he descends, in need of air
To cure his dizziness,
Down past the shipsunk emptiness
Of grownup children's rooms and hallways where
The family portraits blindly stare,
All haunted by each other's likenesses.

Outside, the orchard and a piece of moon
Are islands, he an island as he walks,
Brushing against weed stalks.
By hook and plume
The seeds gathering on his trouser legs

Are archipelagoes, like nests he sees
Shadowed in branching, ramifying trees,
Each with unique expressions in its eggs.
Different islands conjure
Different beings; different beings call
From different isles. And after all
His scrutiny of Nature
All he can see
Is how it will grow small, fade, disappear,
A coastline fading from a traveler
Aboard a survey ship. Slowly,
As coasts depart,
Nature had left behind a naturalist
Bound for a place where species don't exist,
Where no emergence has a counterpart.

He's heard from friends
About the other night, the banquet hall
Ringing with bravos—like a curtain call,
He thinks, when the performance ends,
Failing to summon from the wings
An actor who had lost his taste for verse,
Having beheld, in larger theaters,
Much greater banquet-vanishings
Without the quaint device and thunderclap
Required in Act 3.
He wrote, Let your indulgence set me free,
To the Academy, and took a nap
Beneath a London Daily tent,
Then puttered on his hothouse walk
Watching his orchids beautifully stalk
Their unreturning paths, where each descendant
Is the last—

Their inner staircases
Haunted by vanished insect faces
So tiny, so intolerably vast.
And, while they gave his proxy the award,
He dined in Downe and stayed up rather late
For backgammon with his beloved mate
Who reads his books and is, quite frankly, bored.

Now, done with beetle jaws and beaks of gulls
And bivalve hinges, now, utterly done,
One miracle remains, and only one.
An ocean swell of sickness rushes, pulls,
He leans against the fence
And lights a cigarette and deeply draws,
Done with fixed laws,
Done with experiments
Within his greenhouse heaven where
His offspring, Frank, for half the afternoon
Played, like an awkward angel, his bassoon
Into the humid air
So he could tell
If sound would make a Venus's-Flytrap close.
And, done for good with scientific prose,
That raging hell
Of tortured grammars writhing on their stakes,

He'd turned to his memoirs, chuckling to write
About his boyhood in an upright
Home: a boy preferring gartersnakes
To schoolwork, a lazy, strutting liar
Who quite provoked her aggravated look,
Shushed in the drawingroom behind her book,
His bossy sister itching with desire

To tattletale—yes, that was good.
But even then, much like the conjurer
Grown cranky with impatience to abjure
All his gigantic works and livelihood
In order to immerse
Himself in tales where he could be the man
In Once upon a time there was a man,

He'd quite by chance beheld the universe:
A disregarded game of chess
Between two love-dazed heirs
Who fiddle with the tiny pairs
Of statues in their hands, while numberless
Abstract unseen
Combinings on the silent board remain
Unplayed forever when they leave the game
To turn, themselves, into a king and queen.
Now, like the coming day,
Inhaled smoke illuminates his nerves.
He turns, taking the sandwalk as it curves
Back to the yard, the house, the entrance way
Where, not to waken her,

He softly shuts the door,
And leans against it for a spell before
He climbs the stairs, holding the banister,
Up to their room: there
Emma sleeps, moored
In illusion, blown past the storm he conjured
With his book, into a harbor
Where it all comes clear,
Where island beings leap from shape to shape
As to escape

Their terrifying turns to disappear.
He lies down on the quilt,
He lies down like a fabulous-headed
Fossil in a vanished riverbed,
In ocean-drifts, in canyon floors, in silt,
In lime, in deepening blue ice,
In cliffs obscured as clouds gather and float;
He lies down in his boots and overcoat,
And shuts his eyes.

19 HADLEY STREET

*Even the swallow has found a nest
for herself, near your altar,
O Lord my God.*

1. Dusting

A circle widens beneath my cloth, the years
Of dust rubbed from the wavy windowpanes.
Bits of planets, burst stars have sifted down,
Dust from remote globes of the universe
Drops in our closets, piles in corners softly,
Swirls in sunrays toward boxes we'll unpack,
Around the clocks and mirrors under sheets;
The clouds I shake from carpets give it back,

The children paste paper stars upon the door.
With wet footprints disappearing in the hall,
Old wallpaper designs disclosing faces,
The faucet's voices and the floorboard's cry
Under my heel, what ghost is it accounts
For breath in the rooms, pale tears coursing
The windowpanes, what ghosts? I count even
The doorknob in my hand among the living.

2. *Elizabeth and Eban, 1960*

The windows framed her, watching, and the doors:
Here she was born, she brought her husband here
And loved him, lived with him through two
    world wars,
Ignorant as he was, ox-strong, eyes clear
As water, simple, tender, handy, Christian.
After they found out, he rarely spoke,
She drove him home after the operation.
He sweated through the sheets that night, then woke

And dressed, and watched her make their
    morning coffee.
He sharpened a pencil with a kitchen knife,
Letting the shavings curl around his feet,
And began to write a letter to his wife,

But lowered his head, instead, onto the table.

His heart swished with her nightgown on the floor.
He thought, In this house I have spent most of
My life. It's April. I am sixty-four,
And I have cancer . . . tries not to think, thinks of
His terror bayed in her deep white branches,
His breath vanishing in clouds white as her hair,
The floor's familiar stain, but he blanches
Seeing the stain, a dead man outlined there,
The house outliving him and all its dead.
It didn't matter anymore, but one
Could choose at last, could choose to hold his head,
Or stare into the mirror. Or use a gun.

***

Pages whisper, she turns to John: 16.
A moth beats small wings on the blank ceiling.
Her hand moves to her hair. The windows gleam.
Two years tonight. Outside, the stars keep shining.
Radiators knock, things rustle in the hedge.
She leans over her book, and there God leads
His animals to the purple water's edge
To die of thirst, she sees them as she reads,
The words like bones along the river banks.
She turns the light out and the house is black.
She sits holding her book, no prayers, no thanks
To give. The voiceless fear she fears comes back,
A bird, stripped to its bones, that cannot speak
For holding its own feathers in its beak.

3. *Elizabeth and Eban, 1940*

He watered brickbordered flowerbeds Saturday
And mowed and raked the lawn and weeded it,
Grass settling in his trouser cuffs and shoes.
She talked to him as she stood at the clothesline
Gathering his empty clothes into her arms,
Then swept, dusted, and baked, went shopping for
The Sunday dinner that they served today.
Their next door neighbors came, their Minister
Arrived promptly with flowers at one o'clock:
Lace tablecloth on gleaming mahogany,
Silver candlesticks, a bowl of polished fruit,
Pot roast with rich gravy, and mashed potatoes,
Applesauce, hot biscuits with raspberry jam,
Butter beans, ice water in cut glass goblets,
The Chocolate Lovelight cake she's famous for,
And fresh hot coffee. The widower Johnson's
Square red face beneath white hair grew worried
That the pastor's wife might ask him what he thought
Of the sermon text her husband chose that day,
'Then said the trees unto the bramble, Come thou,
Reign over us,' so he drew a breath
And offered his views of a town selectman:
'As for Williams, he's so broad he's flat.'

The guests are gone now and, the dishes done,
They're in the living room, sitting within
The circle of the lamp. The evening steals
Over their windows, as over a pond.
Outside, June's tree toads peep; she talks
Softly, abstractedly running her hands
Over her stockings, straightening the seams.

His eyes darken looking at her amid
The sprays of rosebuds on their wallpaper,
The roses in their carpet. The hall clock whirs.
And on the small round table at her elbow
Their wedding photograph keeps under glass,
A young couple cutting their wedding cake.
Next to the photo sits a crystal bowl
Of water and white rocks where angelfish
Keep rising to a surface they can't break.

4. *Summer Evening*

Footpaths shine in wet grass, the empty paths,
Black raspberries, apple scent, pears in the trees,
The roses' sleeping heads white on their leaves,
Small caterpillars slowly wave their horns.
Here little moves, but, like a swan, the moon
Riffles the surface, trails night in its wake.
On the lake's floor, this lawn, these trees,
These rooms, these lovers, lie under a spell,
Lie in darkness and find the dark enough.
Indolent dusk, look down, and envy me,
For I have married one with whom I'd lie
Until the vines grew up around our table,
Around our bed as if it were a tower
Guarding our sleep, where whistling birds alight,
Peace be within thy walls, prosperity
Within thy palaces —our walls and rooms
Enthralled by deep drugged vines and
        heartshaped leaves
Where love-sick evening gathers, hangs, and grieves.

5. *Elizabeth, 1905*

Elizabeth bounces like a small white moth
Across the lawn, settling beneath a tree
To stitch her square of half-embroidered cloth,
Embroidering a house and family.
In blue and pink, words stream across the skies,
GOD BLESS OUR HOME. The movement of her eyes,
The motion of her arm pulling the thread.
She is one with the little girl she sewed.
Above her bent and concentrating head
The hundred-year-old pear tree's buds explode.

6. The Picnic, 1895

The photograph we found under the stair
Must have been dropped and left behind.
It shows our house, looming and white and square,
Late summertime.

A white horse grazes, three young women pose,
Their hats enormous, sleeves all lace
Blowing in small breezes that lift their clothes
Now here, now there, then chase

Their laughter, blow off things they've said
Like summer hats down hazy lanes.
Out through the open window overhead
Curtains billow like flames.

7. *Thanksgiving Day Downstairs, 1858*

Thanksgiving afternoon, and Charlotte waits
    On one foot, then the other,
    In the doorway: her mother
Eyes the great platters she decorates

With sugared grapes, while cousin Jed debates
    With Pa, slavery and war.
    Through the buffet's glass door
The patterns painted on white dinnerplates,

Blue willow-trees, blue, half-hidden estates,
    Are delicate, and shine.
    She's old enough, at nine,
To set the table that accommodates

The tall uncles Pa sometimes imitates
    To make Ma laugh and scold.
    Charlotte needn't be told,
She knows, she'll whisper to her schoolmates

How each year Aunt Jerusha celebrates
    By drinking sherry
    And blushes red to see
Bachelor Moody, hat in hand, opening the gates.

8. *Thanksgiving Day Upstairs, 1858*

Charles hears chairs scrape, familiar table prayers,
The clink of glass and silverware downstairs.
He watches patterns on the windows freeze.
Under the heavy blankets, his bent knees
Are mountain peaks, his feet volcanic isles,
The bed a thousand unexplored square miles
Of valleys, meadows—he balances on his lap
His precious atlas, opened to a map
Of North America. His frail, thin fingers
Hover over the continents, he lingers
Sea by sea, turning the wide blue pages.
He raids the coast, his men agree he wages
An astonishing campaign, sailing the covers
Beyond the book-edges where he discovers
The white unbroken stretch of polar cold,
The green heat where the Holy Temple stands.
He looms over his maps, loving to hold
The wide world, like a story, in his hands.

But dear blue boy, you gave a stone a name
One hundred years ago, and nothing came
To you except the footsteps like a promise,
Her hand upon your forehead, and the kiss
Familiar as the blankets you threw off
In sleep's red fever, and your burning cough,
Your dinner trays, your atlas, and your bed,
And secret tears for lives you would have led.

9. *The Living Room*

We've hung David's *La Vierge et Les Saintes*
Near the piano. The companionable blessed
Surround the Virgin, her eyes are tolerant,
Dull with fulfillment. She is perfectly dressed,
Silk sleeves, green velvet gown, and jeweled cap;
Waves cascade down her back. Her Book of Hours,
Unlatched and lying open on her lap
Reveals white, distant, miniature towers
Against a sky of pure, medieval blue,
Rude peasants worshipping, broad fields of wheat
Beneath the sun, moon, stars. A courtly zoo
Feeds in the letters, magnified, ornate,
The lion, monkey, fox, and snakes twining
Around the words amuse her. She chooses not
To read just now, but touches her wedding ring,
And round her waist a gold rope in a knot.
From where she sits, her eyes rest on the keys,
Watching my hands at practice. She enjoys
Bach in Heaven, his sacred Fantasies
For her alone spin like fabulous toys.
Lines shift and break, she finds it rich and right,
Such music out of black dots on the page,
Symbols, the world a symbol from her height,
Great voices rising like smoke from time's wreckage.

Bach, like an epoch, at his clavichord,
Paused listening, and shaking the great head
He watched his mind begin, pressing a chord.
Tonight he would compose. Upstairs in bed
Anna Magdalyn worried, one o'clock
And him so tired, straining the clouded eyes to

Blindness; blindly for hours the master shook
The notes like legible blood-drops onto
The page, Europe a small book in his palm,
Giants in history's pages: 'Study Bach,
There you'll find everything.' And he worked on,
His wife awoke the first on earth to hear
These silver lines beginning, plucked, revolved,
Unearthly trills spiraling up the stair,
The night dispelled, Leipzig itself dissolved,
And Paradise a figuring of air.

10.   *The End of the World, 1843*

'And now the curtain shall be torn
And set on fire and tossed onto
The kindling sticks and rags of Earth:
Blow, Gabriel, to melt your horn!'
That year old women's rumors flew,
Harlots had given monsters birth,

Words in the clouds declared the hundred
Signs, locusts and toads, red skies
Like fire and blood; a fevered wind
Was heard to warn the mighty dead
To gather up their bones and rise;
Young girls saw flocks of angels in

The autumn trees, waiting. At night
Each girl sewed her Ascension Gown,
The women gathered at the well—
Their faces shone with wondrous light
Since William Miller came to town
And pitched a tent, preaching of hell

With paper strips of published facts:
'Began B. C. 457,
Ends in 1843.
Children of darkness, your dark acts,
Dark words and thoughts, have angered Heaven!'
The townsfolk listened solemnly,

Went to the graveyard to await
On consecrated plots of ground
The horrible blast that would destroy,
Unspeakably, their low estate.
They waited for the furious sound
Week after week, until a boy

Impatiently climbed up on the roof
Of 19 Hadley Street and pressed
His tin horn to his lips and blew:
For Comfort Ferry it was proof
The world had ended, and he blessed
Himself before he swooned and grew

A nasty goose-egg on his head;
And Esmerrianna Knott
Listened, then calmly bent to close
Her hem up with a gathering thread
So sinners left on earth could not
Look up her dress as she arose.

11. *Halloween*

The children's room glows radiantly by
The light of pumpkins on the windowsill
That fiercely grin on sleeping boy and girl.
She stirs and mutters in her sleep, Goodbye,

Who scared herself a little in a sheet
And walked the streets with devils and dinosaurs
And bleeping green men flown from distant stars.
We sit up late, and smoke, and talk about

Our awkward, loving Frankenstein in bed
Who told his sister that it isn't true,
That real men in real boxes never do
Haunt houses. But the King of the Dead

Has taken off his mask tonight, and twirled
His cape and vanished, and we are his
Who know beyond all doubt how real he is:
Out of his bag of sweets he plucks the world.

12. *Samuel Judd, 1820*

You didn't know your date of birth, you said;
Some swore that you were older than the flood.
You'd bare discolored teeth, shaking your head,
And curse like summer thunder, Samuel Judd.

Still, to see you toiling down the stair,
Or standing crooked at your crooked door,
Or on the front porch in your rocking chair,
One wouldn't know that you were hard at war:

You tied tin cans on strings for your alarms.
You'd doze, the Good Book sliding from your knees,
And at a sound you'd jump, flapping your arms
To scare off children from your apple trees.

13. The Paperweight

The scene within the paperweight is calm,
A small white house, a laughing man and wife,
Deep snow. I turn it over in my palm
And watch it snowing in another life,

Another world, and from this scene learn what
It is to stand apart: she serves him tea
Once and forever, dressed from head to foot
As she is always dressed. In this toy, history

Comes down in the dark like snow, and we
Wonder if her single deed tells much
Or little of the way she loves, and whether he
Sees shadows in the sky. Beyond our touch,

Beyond our lives, they laugh, and drink their tea.
We look at them just as the winter night
With its vast empty spaces bends to see
Our isolated little world of light,

Covered with snow, and snow in clouds above it,
And drifts and swirls too deep to understand.
Still, I must try to think a little of it,
With so much winter in my head and hand.

14. *The Parsonage, 1785*

Reverend Eliphet Swift, man of the Lord,
Your parish crowded our frontrooms, parlors, halls,
For wakes and weddings. Your letters record
So many shad swarming South Hadley Falls
That as you rowed you struck them with your oars.
You put St. Andrew's cross above each latch
To scare away the witches from your doors,
And from these windows you would stand and watch
Storms break on good and bad, your penitents
Like boulders in the field. You were a rock:
No painted likeness, books, or instruments,
No silver spoons, no mirror, and no clock,
No Salem glassware, no excessive light
From candelabras—let the woman fuss.
Enough for you to have a fire each night,
And spring each year rose green as Lazarus.

Eliphet Swift, you knew why you came West,
Stranding your sisters on the village shores
To Bibles and rising bread, ten, twelve times blest
With child, your mother anxious at her chores,
Your father gone to sea, and in your head
The grey Atlantic swirling and the whale
That smashed a ship, leaving your brother dead.
You kept seeing Leviathan's great tail
Parting the sea like God, black noise, black air.
One hundred miles inland: still you could smell
Fear churning like an ocean in your prayer.
Christ knew the water, chose to row through hell.

You saw the empty shells, bones in the tide,
And fled, yet crucifixes on your walls
Were hulks of whale hanging from His Ship's side.
Your last years found you fishing at the Falls.

15. *The Meeting in the Kitchen, 1740*

Scissors, tallow, sieve and knife,
Balls of twine and weathervanes,
Meadows filled with spadefoot frogs,
Says Cotton Witt has took to wife
A witch, and her alone explains
Our frost of June, our rabid dogs,

Our sickles broke, our oxen drowned.
Spiddy Preston took to bed
With beestings blistering both her arms
After she chased Witt's pigs around
Her flax garden, and now she's dead.

Lord keep the Devil from our farms.

The future opens like a grave
Unless our incantation save
South Hadley from this witch's bite,
Star of Wormwood, Tree of Night.